EXPLODING KITTENS®
A FIELD GUIDE
TO UNUSUAL CATS

Running Press
Hachette Book Group
1290 Avenue of the Americas, New York, NY 10104
www.runningpress.com
@Running_Press

Printed in China

First Edition: June 2020

Published by Running Press, an imprint of Perseus Books, LLC, a subsidiary of Hachette Book Group, Inc. The Running Press name and logo is a trademark of the Hachette Book Group.

The Hachette Speakers Bureau provides a wide range of authors for speaking events. To find out more, go to www.hachettespeakersbureau.com or call (866) 376-6591.

The publisher is not responsible for websites (or their content) that are not owned by the publisher.

Print book cover and interior design by Marissa Raybuck.

Library of Congress Control Number: 2019951022

ISBN: 978-0-7624-9744-7 (hardcover), 978-0-7624-9745-4 (ebook)

1010

10 9 8 7 6 5 4 3 2 1

EXPLODING KITTENS®
A FIELD GUIDE TO UNUSUAL
CATS

EXPLODING KITTENS AND SAM STALL

RUNNING PRESS
PHILADELPHIA

CONTENTS

———

INTRODUCTION (AND WARNING)

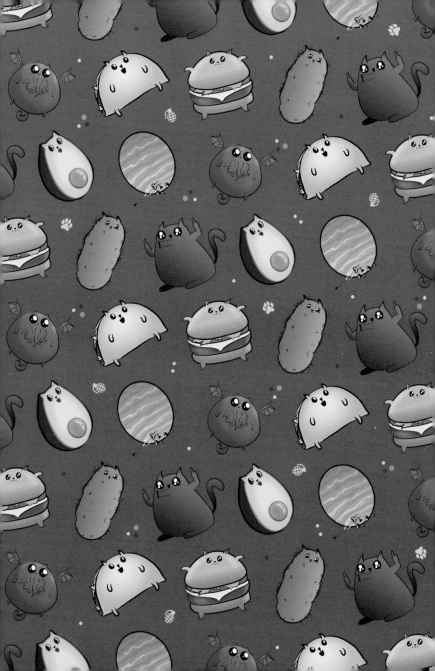

It wasn't so long ago that the only people interested in Exploding Kittens were cat breeders and ordinance experts. But, recently, the general public has become fascinated with these captivating creatures, many of which possess the powers to defy the laws of biology, physics, and even common sense.

Unlike conventional felines, which confine their activities to eating, sleeping, and disgorging the occasional hairball, Exploding Kittens can (among a great many other things) fly, swim, predict the future, wield weapons like swords, and pilot armored vehicles. And, of course, some of them explode.

Clearly, we are not dealing with typical cats here. Which is why we have painstakingly prepared, for the first time ever, this essential field guide to better inform enthusiastic but unsuspecting potential owners about each breed's fortes and foibles.

On the following pages we introduce you to forty of the most well-known Exploding Kitten varieties. Why does the Rainbow-Ralphing Cat vomit rainbows? How does one grow a Cattermelon? And is it safe to keep a Catnado in a trailer park? (No, it isn't.) Learn all this and more.

Remember, no Exploding Kittens were harmed in the making of this book. Though the same cannot be said for its editor, whose left pinkie was preternaturally lopped off by a Sword Cat. We're only a little bit sorry.

CATEGORIES

FOR YOUR SAFETY AND CONVENIENCE, EACH CAT PROFILE OFFERS MUCH (BUT NOT ALL) OF THE FOLLOWING INFORMATION.

ORIGIN
How did this creature come to be?

PHYSICAL CHARACTERISTICS
What color are they? How much do they weigh? Can they fly, swim, or travel in space?

BEHAVIOR
Does your favorite cat suffer from a shy bladder, or lead a dangerous double life?

BREEDING
Do they procreate in the usual way, or via seeds or asexual division? Or can they reproduce at all?

WHERE TO FIND THEM
These cats aren't exactly pet store staples. Places frequented by the various Exploding Kittens breeds.

WHERE *NOT* TO FIND THEM
Some paths are best left untraveled.

BENEFITS
Positive attributes, from the gift of prophecy to lawn-care skills.

HOME CARE TIP
Catering to your pet's bizarre, even terrifying, needs.

HEALTH
What physical issues (besides exploding) should you worry about?

GROOMING
The best ways to keep your cat in tip-top condition.

USES
A few varieties are actually quite helpful around the house.

FUN FACT
Often amusing, occasionally worrisome, tidbits about particular breeds.

WARNING
For some of these cats, the ever-present threat of spontaneous explosions isn't their only (or even their worst) drawback.

WHICH CAT IS RIGHT FOR YOU?

LOOKING FOR A SPECIFIC KIND OF EXPLODING KITTEN? WE'VE DIVIDED THEM UP BASED ON THEIR MOST PREVALENT TRAITS.

ATHLETIC

If your idea of a fun morning is a five-mile run, consider the Helicatpter (page 056), which can easily match your pace, thanks to the three-foot-long rotors on its head. Or say Namaste to the absurdly flexible Yoga Cat (page 088).

SEDENTARY

Couch potatoes can try the Avocato (page 016), the Hairy Potato Cat (page 024), or the Cattermelon (page 022). They don't just dislike exercise; they're physically incapable of doing it.

DANGEROUS

Read about the lava-spitting Volcato (page 070) or the trailer park–leveling Catnado (page 068).

EXTREMELY DANGEROUS

If you're not afraid of a slow, painful demise, consider the bloodthirsty Great White Cat (page 044), or the planet-devouring majesty of the Imploding Kitten (page 042).

BAD

Lock up your belongings and consider taking in an Imposter Cat (page 058).

ATTENTION-GRABBING

Hit the beach with Bikini Cat (page 076), sulk artfully with Emo Emu Cat (page 078), or boost your facial hair game with Beard Cat (page 074).

FOOD-THEMED

Numerous breeds are as succulent-sounding as they are cute. There's the burger-like Royale with Fleas (page 028), the warm and sweet Catpuccino (page 020), the always approachable Catifornia Roll (page 018), and the festive Tacocat (page 032). Warning: All these cats are, in fact, inedible.

WEIRD

Try Rainbow-Ralphing Cat (page 062). Full stop. Seriously, this cat spits rainbows—it's got "weird" totally covered.

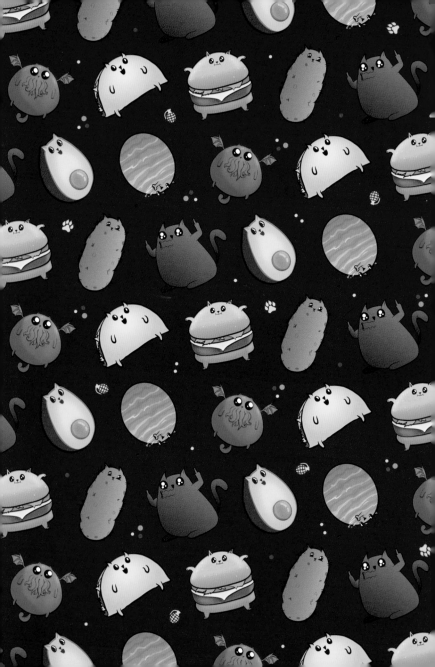

THE EXPLODING KITTENS

CATS

THAT LOOK LIKE FOOD

AVOCATO

AVOCADO CATTUS

ORIGIN

The Avocato got its start more than a millennium ago in Central America, when Mesoamerican farmers, fresh from their successful domestication of corn, decided to kick things up a notch by crossing the native avocado plant with an ocelot.

PHYSICAL CHARACTERISTICS

Roughly the same size and shape as a hand grenade, its flesh is extremely firm and resilient during youth, but grows ever mushier with age.

HEALTH

Bruises easily, and typically has a very short life span. However, its days can be extended by bathing in lemon juice.

BREEDING

The population is slowly declining because each Avocato only produces a single, absurdly large seed during its lifetime.

HOME CARE TIP

There's nothing an Avocato enjoys more than lounging on a piece of toast.

CATIFORNIA ROLL

RICE ET CATTUS PISCIS

ORIGIN

The Catifornia Roll was first introduced to US cat fanciers during the 1970s when the tightly wrapped, cylindrical breed started appearing in select Japanese restaurants.

PHYSICAL CHARACTERISTICS

Casual observers might notice that a streak of Avocato (page 016) runs through the Catifornia Roll.

BEHAVIOR

Normally mild and unchallenging. However, the breed can become quite a handful if exposed to wasabi.

WHERE TO FIND THEM

Hanging out at pretty much any Japanese eatery, usually in great numbers.

WHERE NOT TO FIND THEM

Vending machines. Sketchy-looking convenience stores. Restaurants that have recently suffered power outages.

CATPUCCINO

CAPULUS CATTUS

ORIGIN

When it was first brought to Europe from the Americas in the early sixteenth century, the Catpuccino was infamous for its bold personality and pitch-black coat. But after a group of Capuchin friars took an interest in the breed, it gradually became the milder, frothier, lighter-colored pet that's popular all over the world today.

PHYSICAL CHARACTERISTICS

A little on the small side. Some sport whimsical designs on their backs—most commonly hearts.

WARNING

Given the Catpuccino's small size and agreeable nature, it's tempting to get a second one. And perhaps a third. Resist this urge, because having too many Catpuccinos can trigger nervousness and insomnia.

FUN FACT

Like most cats, the Catpuccino enjoys a saucer of milk. *Unlike* most cats, it prefers it steamed and foamed.

CATTERMELON

CUCUMIS CATTUS

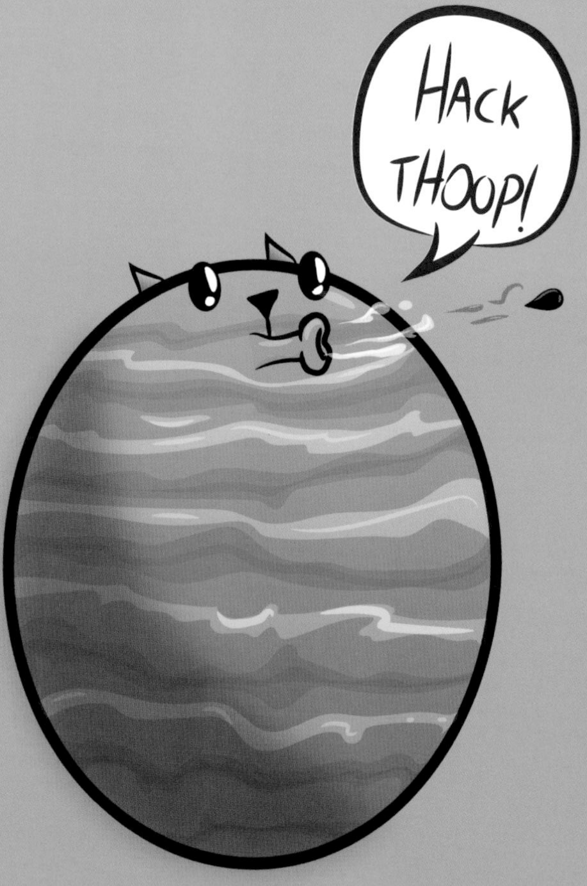
HACK THOOP!

ORIGIN

Cattermelon was born in a secret government facility that used gene splicing to create weaponized versions of common fruits and vegetables. They grow from seeds, making them the only feline commonly sold at garden centers. Behavior: One of the few feline types that's entirely uninterested in climbing. Mostly because a fall from higher than four feet will splatter them.

BREEDING

Cattermelons cannot be crossbred with other fruit-based feline breeds, such as the Avocato (page 016). If you don't wish to breed your Cattermelon at all, a seedless variety is available.

HAIRY POTATO CAT

**CAPSICUM ANNUUM MOREM PELLIS
HISPIDUS CATTUS**

ORIGIN

Imported from North America to Ireland in the sixteenth century, refined by cat breeders in the Emerald Isle, and then sent back to North America, this nondescript feline certainly wins no awards for its looks. Or athleticism. Or intelligence. However, it's definitely low maintenance, requiring nothing from its owner beyond a cool, quiet corner in the root cellar.

BEHAVIOR

All but incapable of independent movement, it spends its days staring vacantly into space and shedding relentlessly.

FUN FACT

Develops extra eyes as it ages.

WHERE TO FIND THEM

Idaho.

WHERE NOT TO FIND THEM

In heavily compressed soils with poor drainage and little organic matter.

HAIRY POTATO CAT — CAPSICUM ANNUUM MOREM PELLIS HISPIDUS CATTUS

KITTYCHANGA

FABA QUOQUE SAGINATI CATTUS

ORIGIN

A native, like the Tacocat (page 032), of the Texas/
Mexico borderlands, the Kittychanga has internal organs
protected by a hard carapace made from a deep-fried
flour tortilla.

BEHAVIOR

A festive, happy feline that pretty much everyone loves
to have around. Some specimens, however, can be a bit
tightly wrapped.

HEALTH

Never overstuff your Kittychanga. Too much food can
cause a Kittychanga's shell to burst.

HOME CARE TIP

At night, Kittychangas love to rest on a bed of lettuce.
Owning multiple members of the breed is easy, because
they stack together quite nicely.

ROYALE
WITH FLEAS

REGALEM CUM PULICIBUS

ORIGIN

This tubby little feline, with its fluffy, bunlike body and appetizing aroma, has been one of America's top breeds for decades—though it's recently lost ground to the Tacocat (page 032) and the Kittychanga (page 026).

PHYSICAL CHARACTERISTICS

Available in two major varieties: sesame seed bun and regular bun. A vegetarian Royale with Fleas recently appeared, but fans of the traditional breed complain that it "just isn't the same."

HEALTH

In spite of its name, the Royale with Fleas doesn't actually carry these bloodsucking parasites. It is, however, absolutely chock-full of cholesterol and sodium.

BREEDING

The Royale's tiny kittens are known as "sliders."

SOUR PUSS

PUSS UVAM

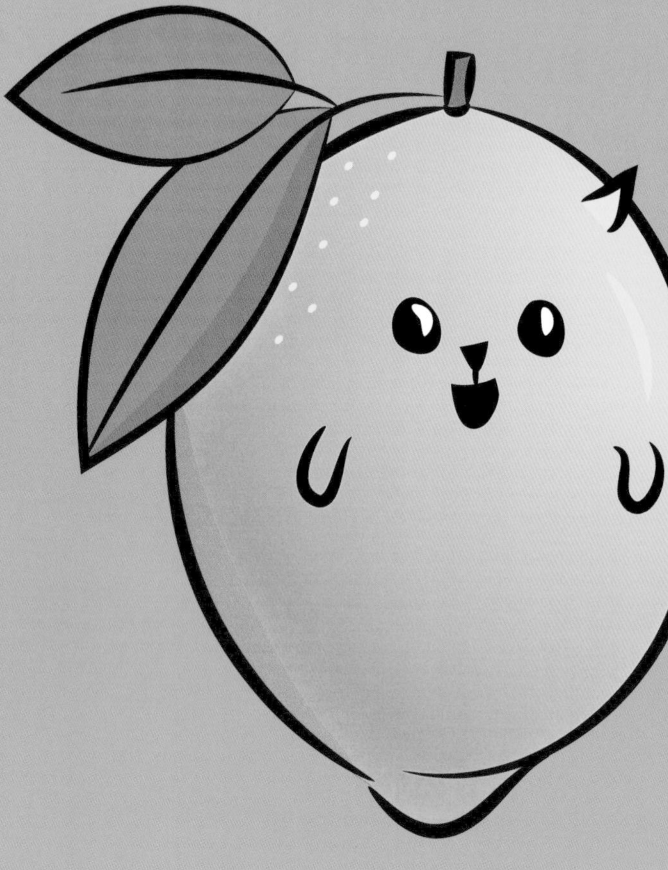

ORIGIN

First bred on the sunny plains of southern Spain, the
Sour Puss melds cat characteristics with those of the
lemon. It's now popular the world over as a living,
purring air freshener.

PHYSICAL CHARACTERISTICS

The Sour Puss looks much more like a lemon than a cat.
Most spend their entire lives attached to their host Sour
Puss trees, swaying in the breeze and futilely swatting at
passing insects.

BEHAVIOR

In spite of its name, the Sour Puss is actually quite cheerful,
sporting a broad smile and an agreeable disposition.

HEALTH

Though the typical Sour Puss looks defenseless, they, in
fact, have little to fear in the wild. Their internal juices are
so bitter that no predators dare bite them.

HOME CARE TIP

Because they lack any fur to speak of, grooming is easy.
Just wipe them off occasionally to remove dust.

TACOCAT

TACO CATTUS

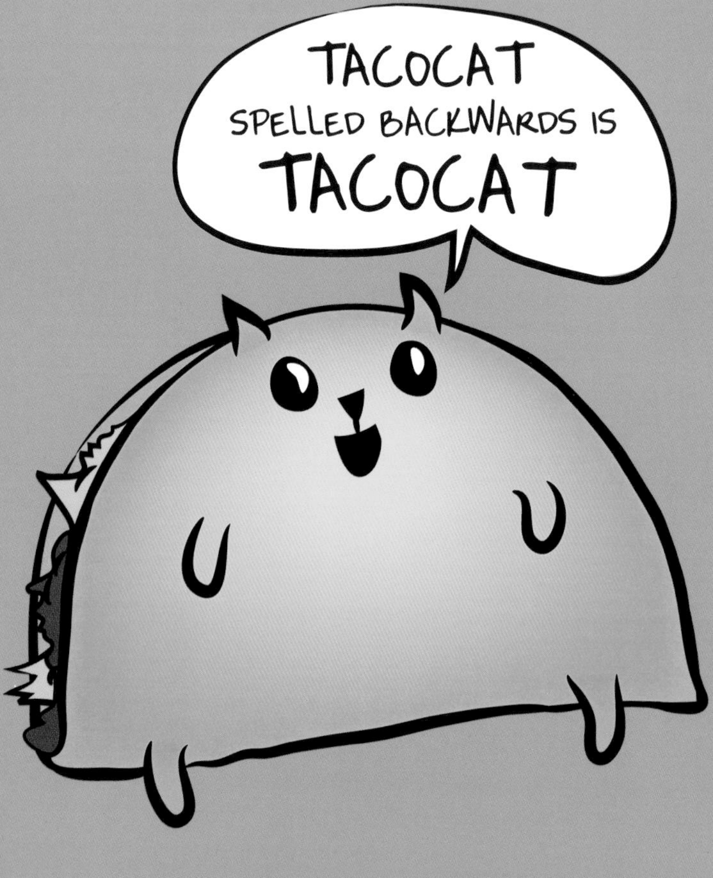
TACOCAT
SPELLED BACKWARDS IS
TACOCAT

ORIGIN

Over the last few decades this denizen of the United States/Mexico border region has grown vastly in popularity. However, Mexican experts say it bears little resemblance to the country's other indigenous breeds, such as the Avocato (page 016), while US authorities consider its proliferation a threat to native species such as the Royale with Fleas (page 028).

GROOMING

The Tacocat can be extraordinarily messy, leaving behind stray pieces of lettuce and tomato wherever it goes. Owners should invest in a wax paper–lined cat bed.

BREEDING

Commonly producing litters of six and up to a dozen kittens, this prolific breed has grown so numerous that animal shelters often hold Tacocat Tuesdays in an effort to find homes for strays.

ZUKITTY

CAT CUCURBITA

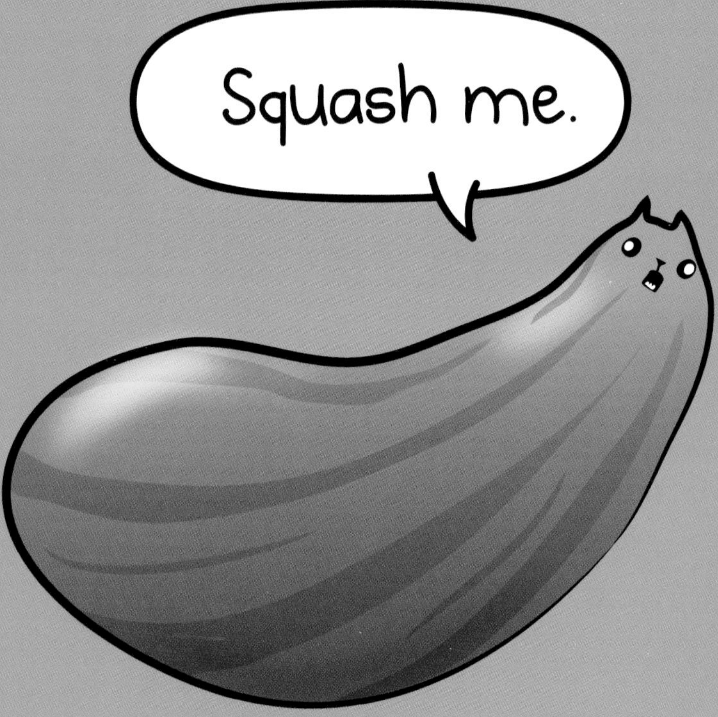
Squash me.

ORIGIN

Unlike the Cattermelon (page 022), which is a product of twenty-first-century genetic engineering, the ZuKitty came about through a romantic liaison between a cat and a plant—the less of which we know about, the better.

PHYSICAL CHARACTERISTICS

ZuKitties are large, fleshy, oblong creatures with green/white skin and the facial features of a cat. They get along with pretty much every other feline breed, mostly because in fights they can neither defend themselves nor run away.

BREEDING

Plant ZuKitty seeds in late spring, after all danger of frost has passed. If left too long on the vine, they can grow to the size of mountain lions. The average litter from a single ZuKitty vine can exceed two hundred kittens.

USES

None. In fact, most gardeners/cat breeders regret wasting the prodigious garden space necessary to host even one ZuKitty vine.

NOT SAFE FOR WORK
CATS

CATHULU

VETUS UNUS MAGNA

ORIGIN

It is said that one day this eldritch extradimensional entity will awaken from its eons-long catnap and sweep away reality like a feline smacking knickknacks off an end table. Certain ancient texts hint darkly at the primordial origins of Dread Cathulu, but anyone who attempts to read them instantly goes mad.

PHYSICAL CHARACTERISTICS

Unknown, because none may look upon Cathulu's true form and live.

BEHAVIOR

Like all felines, Cathulu does pretty much whatever Cathulu wants. Unfortunately for us, all he wants to do is sow chaos, despair, and death.

WHERE TO FIND HIM

You really, really don't want to find him. However, if you insist, first open an interdimensional portal to the hellish plane of existence where he resides. Then turn on an electric can opener and let it run for a few seconds. Cathulu will come. And when he does, there had better be some Seafood Mixed Grill waiting for him.

GREAT WHITE CAT

MAGNUS ALBUS FELES

ORIGIN

All cats adore fish, but only the Great White possesses
the tools to acquire this delicacy on its own, without
relying on humans and their can openers.

PHYSICAL CHARACTERISTICS

Can reach more than twenty feet in length, making it
an impractical pet for all but the most dedicated home
aquarium enthusiasts. They are, however, extremely
popular with supervillains.

FUN FACT

While many marine predators hunt in schools, Great
Whites (in a nod to their feline ancestry) refuse to
cooperate with each other in any way.

IMPLODING KITTEN

CONTRAHENDIS CATALUS

ORIGIN

Born shortly after the creation of the universe and composed of highly compacted matter from the hearts of collapsed stars, Imploding Kittens generate gravitational fields capable of capturing and consuming entire planets.

WARNING

They make poor house pets, because even small specimens exceed more than three astronomical units in size. Also, the Imploding Kitten is so long-lived that it will probably still exist after every star in the known universe expends its nuclear fuel and burns out. Only the most committed pet owners need apply.

BEHAVIOR

Will never come when you want them to. However, given their irresistible gravitational attraction, *you* will definitely come when *they* want you to.

HEALTH

Food intake should be carefully monitored; left to their own devices, Imploding Kittens will consume literally anything.

SWORD KITTEN

CATALUS GLADIO

ORIGIN

After an unsuccessful attempt to breed a "guard cat,"
this formidable swordsman refuses to employ his skills
for home defense or the protection of his master. Instead,
he uses his blade with great vigor against upholstered
sofas and chairs.

BEHAVIOR

The Sword Kitten loves nothing more than to cross swords
with other Exploding Kittens. They will (unless prevented)
conduct such duels while scrambling across a steep roof,
teetering on the railing of a high-rise balcony, or standing
far too close to the edge of a tall cliff.

FUN FACT

Most Sword Kittens are named Blade, D'Artagnan,
or Zorro.

TANK CAT

CATTUS LORICATORUM

ORIGIN

Tank Cats, first deployed during the Cold War, were once considered a highly versatile weapon. However, their tendency to go haywire at the sight of laser-guided weapons (and lasers in general) has relegated them to training and mascot duties.

PHYSICAL CHARACTERISTICS

Tank Cats drive the tiny Mark E Overland War Wagon, or MEOWW. Though barely bigger than a Roomba, the vehicle can nevertheless reach forty miles an hour in open country and lay down a withering barrage with its 20mm canon.

BENEFITS

Excellent for home defense.

GROOMING

All cats are neat and fastidious, but the Tank Cat, thanks to its Army basic training, takes this to the next level. This is the only breed that both trims its own claws and changes its own litter pan.

USES

Retired Tank Cats often find employment as lawn mowers and Uber drivers.

ZOMBIE CAT

CATTUS MORTUUS VIVENTEM

ORIGIN

No one's sure where they come from, but pretty much everybody wishes these undead abominations would go away.

PHYSICAL CHARACTERISTICS

Available in green, bluish green, and (in later stages of decomposition) gray.

GROOMING

Refrain from bathing your Zombie Cat. It does nothing to dampen their inherent gaminess, and may accelerate decomposition. Instead, tie a car deodorizer to its collar.

BREEDING

Zombie Cats are incapable of conventional procreation. However, they can "turn" other felines by biting them—which they will do with great zeal if given the chance. Please keep yours indoors.

HEALTH

The breed, being clinically dead, is beyond conventional health concerns. If a limb or tail falls off, reattach it with duct tape.

STRANGE
BUT TRUE
CATS

CAT WIZARD

NEC DIVINOS CATTUS

ORIGIN

Myriad cultures tell tales of a mystical feline sage whose gift of prophecy guided great warriors and prophets throughout the centuries. Unfortunately, in order to gain the Cat Wizard's powers of prescience, those heroes had to do something very unheroic: stare intently at its butt.

PHYSICAL CHARACTERISTICS

The Cat Wizard is said to look extremely ancient, with a facial beard (unusual, but not unheard of in felines) and a pointy hat.

WHERE TO FIND THEM

When the brave seek wise counsel, it will be there. When the ignorant quest for knowledge, it will be there. But if you're trying to, say, pick next week's winning lottery digits, it definitely *won't* be there. The Cat Wizard doesn't use its magical backside for frivolous ends.

FUN FACT

Some believe Cat Wizard coined the phrase "Hindsight is 20/20."

FERAL CAT

CURET CATTUS

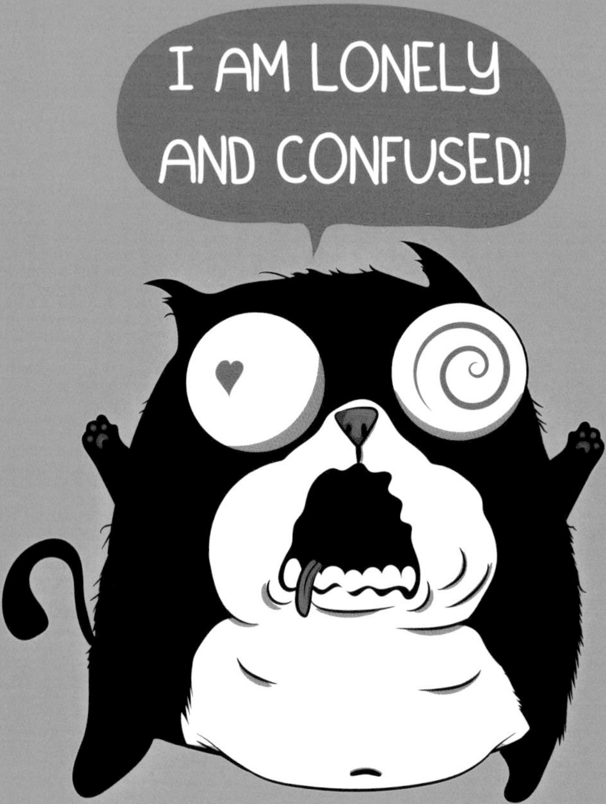
I AM LONELY
AND CONFUSED!

ORIGIN

By far one of the most numerous of all the bizarre breeds featured in this book. That's because it wasn't created to serve a purpose. It's a mishmash of all the felines who were, at some point, either lost or simply discarded.

PHYSICAL CHARACTERISTICS

The typical Feral Cat can look like anything. Name a genetic combination, and chances are it already lurks in a vacant lot near you.

HEALTH

Not great. It's understandable, given that, for a feral cat, "getting something to eat" often means fighting a raccoon for a discarded sack of French fries.

BREEDING

If Feral Cats have a superpower, it's reproduction. The typical female produces fifteen litters of approximately ten kittens each annually. If she lives for ten years (quite an achievement for a Feral Cat), she'll produce more than fifteen hundred offspring.

HELICATPTER

CATTUS VOLATILI

ORIGIN

The misguided result of an attempt by the Defense
Advanced Research Projects Agency to give regular
domestic cats the power of flight. Unfortunately, the $2.3
billion program's only tangible product was a new breed
of feline with helicopter blades sticking out of its head.

PHYSICAL CHARACTERISTICS

Fully functional rotors can raise Helicatpters to more than
one hundred feet in altitude and propel them at speeds of
eighty miles per hour.

BEHAVIOR

Somewhat needy. Tend to hover.

BREEDING

Helicatpter parents are quite possessive of their
kittens, obsessing over every aspect of their lives and
often supervising them far into adulthood. Warning:
Helicatpters are not allowed within two statute miles
of any municipal airport.

IMPOSTER CAT

CATTUS SIMULARE

ORIGIN

No one is quite sure where the Imposter Cat comes from, what it wants, what sort of cat it is—or even if it's a cat at all. Authorities first became aware of the breed in 1972, when a New York City jewelry store was robbed by an imposter posing as the shop's beloved mascot, a tabby named Bowser (who was later discovered tied up in a storeroom). Since then, Imposter Cats have been implicated in crimes ranging from bank robberies to elaborate Ponzi schemes.

BEHAVIOR

Furtive and sneaky. For a while it was theorized that Imposter Cats were in fact raccoons, since their thieving ways closely mimic the Trash Panda's modus operandi. However, the items Imposter Cats like to steal, such as cash, jewelry, and bearer bonds, are completely different from the things raccoons favor, such as marshmallows and loaves of moldy bread.

PHYSICAL CHARACTERISTICS

The breed's true face is anyone's guess, since the Imposter Cat is usually garbed in a *Mission Impossible*–quality disguise.

FUN FACT

The Imposter Cat is the only feline breed on Interpol's "Wanted Persons" list.

NOPE KITTEN

NEC CATULUS

ORIGIN

This breed's risk assessment capabilities exceed those of insurance actuaries. Unlike the typical feline, which literally leaps before it looks, the Nope Kitten carefully gauges the dangers of every activity, from skydiving to crossing a lightly traveled road. And if there's even a slight risk to life and limb, it typically finds something better (or at least safer) to do.

PHYSICAL CHARACTERISTICS

Somewhat overweight, thanks to all the activities it refuses to attempt. Its fur comes in all shades, though often with a yellow streak on its back.

HEALTH

Nope Kittens can develop severe tension headaches from constant overthinking.

WHERE TO FIND THEM

At home, hiding under a bed.

WHERE NOT TO FIND THEM

Airplanes, rickety carnival rides, skydiving schools, restaurants cited by the health department, subways at 2 a.m., etc.

RAINBOW-RALPHING CAT

VOMITUS ARCUS MEUS CATTUS

ORIGIN

This breed does exactly what its name implies—
hurls out brilliant, multicolored lighting effects about
as frequently as regular cats puke up hairballs. Though
there's no cleanup involved (the rainbows are just geysers
of electrons), having your cat light up like a New York City
warehouse rave can be disconcerting. Especially when
your Rainbow-Ralphing Cat does it at, say, 2 a.m. on
a Tuesday.

BEHAVIOR

The typical Rainbow-Ralphing Cat has an "incident"
roughly once every hour. You'll know it's time when it
hunkers down and spasms in a rhythm eerily similar to
the opening beat of Daft Punk's iconic "Harder, Better,
Faster, Stronger" track.

HEALTH

Rainbow-Ralphing Cat's achingly bright, unpredictable
light shows make it a very poor choice for cat fanciers
with epilepsy.

WARNING

Rainbow-Ralphing kittens start to exhibit their signature
behavior just days after birth. Which means that, if you
own an adult cat with six kittens, you could face a ralphing
incident every hour on the hour, around the clock.

SHY BLADDER CAT

FUGAX URINARIA CATTUS

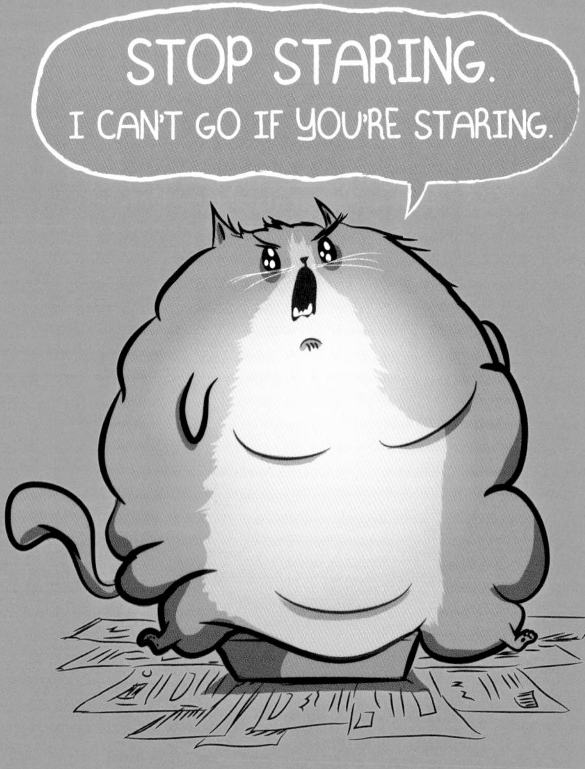
STOP STARING.
I CAN'T GO IF YOU'RE STARING.

ORIGIN

At some point in its evolution this feline developed an intense aversion to public urination. Many specimens even have problems peeing in the privacy of their own litter boxes—especially if they suspect that someone can hear them.

PHYSICAL CHARACTERISTICS

While the typical cat's default facial expression is one of calm indifference, Shy Bladder Cat's is an unnerving mix of frustration and overwhelming need.

HEALTH

Prone to urinary tract infections. Some particularly bashful breeds may require a cat-theter.

WHERE TO FIND THEM

Actually, if you suspect that your Shy Bladder Cat is trying to urinate, it is essential that you *not* try to find them.Walking in on one or calling their name at the critical moment can ruin everything.

WHERE NOT TO FIND THEM

Public restrooms.

TROPICAL
DEPRESSION
CATS

CATNADO

CATTUS TURBINIS VASTI

Calm   TOTAL DEVASTATION   Calm again

ORIGIN

In 1932, an otherwise "normal" Kansas barn cat named Skeeter was sucked into an F1 tornado. Several minutes inside the storm's vortex left him dizzy, somewhat bruised, and with the power to create small whirlwinds simply by running around in tight circles for a minute. Today, his storm-summoning progeny can be found all over America's Great Plains.

BEHAVIOR

Capricious and unpredictable—just like tornados.

WHERE TO FIND THEM

Tornado alley. Every spring, teams of "Catnado chasers," composed of meteorologists and veterinarians, range across the American heartland hoping to encounter and study these felines.

WHERE NOT TO FIND THEM

Trailer parks, most of which ban Catnados.

VOLCATO

MONS IGNEUS CATTUS

ORIGIN

All cats throw up occasionally, but when this breed loses its lunch there's cause for real concern—and perhaps for a mass evacuation. Unlike Rainbow-Ralphing Cat (page 062), which spews forth harmless multicolored light shows, Volcato hurls incandescent strands of molten magma. They're as old as the earth itself, drawing their superheated spew directly from the planet's raging core.

PHYSICAL CHARACTERISTICS

Roughly the size of a "regular" volcano, but sporting a cat's face on its barren, sulfur-coated slopes. Eruptions are usually preceded by earthquakes and what's been described as a "huck-huck" noise.

WARNING

In addition to puking lava, the Volcato is infamous for its flatulence. Their silent but deadly emissions range from caustic acid to foul-smelling sulfur to asphyxiating carbon dioxide—or all three at the same time.

COOL
CATS

BEARD CAT

BARBA CATTUS

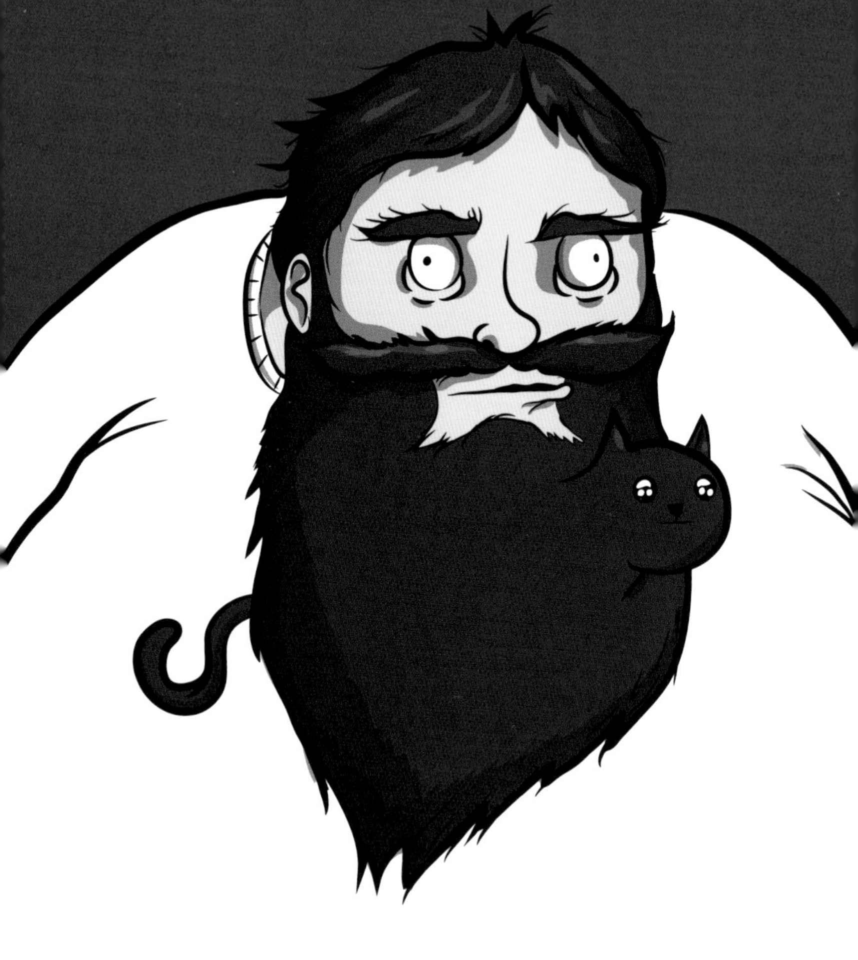

ORIGIN

Over the centuries Beard Cats have been the neck-borne companions of numerous historical figures, including the Russian monk Rasputin, who reportedly hosted four of them in his prodigious facial hair.

PHYSICAL CHARACTERISTICS

The breed rarely weighs more than three or four pounds, lessoning neck strain on its human companions.

BEHAVIOR

Somewhat coarse and prone to scratching.

GROOMING

Your Beard Cat will start to smell like stale dishwater and neck sweat if not regularly brushed and bathed.

BENEFITS

Keeps your face mouse-free!

BIKINI CAT

ADHIBET LATEBRAS CATTUS

ORIGIN

Oddly, the Bikini Cat is far older than the garment after which it is named. Known in the nineteenth century as the Ladies Swimming Costume Cat, this breed formerly prowled the world's beaches in a loose-fitting wool outfit that covered every part of its body except the head and paws. However, its name changed along with social mores and, by the 1970s, the modern Bikini Cat was strutting its stuff from the Copacabana to Saint-Tropez.

PHYSICAL CHARACTERISTICS

Females of the species sport smart-looking swimwear of the latest design. However, males will wear the same pair of faded, knee-length swim trunks year after year, if permitted. In the southern United States they can regularly be seen in jean shorts and (no matter what their age or physical condition) in low-rise Speedos in Europe.

WARNING

Cats poop in sandboxes. The beach is a giant sandbox. Please keep a close eye on your pet.

(EMO) EMU CAT

CATTUS EMU

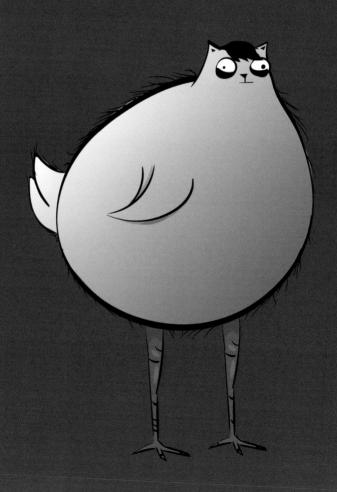

ORIGIN

A couple of centuries ago, an extremely lonely domestic housecat formed an intimate alliance with an emu (the world's second-largest flightless bird). Out of this peculiar union came the Emu Cat, a six-foot-tall hybrid that's become an icon in its Australian homeland. There's also a far less numerous subspecies called the Emo Emu Cat, which is basically an Emu Cat with an edgy hairstyle, black pigment around its eyes, and a cynical attitude.

BEHAVIOR

Emu Cats spend their days running with abandon across the outback. Emo Emu Cats spend their days lurking under shade trees, judging the Emu Cats.

WARNING

Emo Emu Cats can cause painful wounds. Not with the powerful claws on their feet, but with their sarcasm.

KITTEN PRESIDENT

CATTUS PRAESES

ORIGIN

The first representative of this breed was born at the dawn of the nineteenth century in a log cabin on the American frontier. Since then it's thrived by mimicking pretty much every popular cliché about how a proper POTUS should look and behave.

PHYSICAL CHARACTERISTICS

Kitten Presidents are generically attractive shorthairs with whitish fur. They sport furrowed brows and a pursed mouth, which passes for an expression of benign interest and concern—or as close to that as any feline can manage.

BREEDING

Kitten Presidents usually mate for life and often seek out partners who serve as foils to their somewhat staid, serious personalities.

WARNING

During election years, limit your Kitten President's access to social media and cable TV news. Too much polling data and political commentary make them anxious.

LUMBER CAT

LIGNA CATTUS

ORIGIN

Produced more than a century ago by crossing
domestic cats with the Canadian lynx, this burly breed
quickly found work in lumber camps, hunting mice. And
also rats, wolverines, badgers, cougars, bald eagles,
grizzly bears, and anything else dumb enough to mess
with it. They also somehow acquired small axes, which
they employ both in their animal control duties, and to
chop down the occasional pine or spruce.

PHYSICAL CHARACTERISTICS

Its upper-body fur sports a red-and-black plaid pattern,
and the top of its head is covered in tightly woven hair
that resembles a toque.

WHERE TO FIND THEM

The misty, trackless forests of the Canadian Northwest.
Or, if it's breakfast time, the nearest Tim Hortons.

FUN FACT

To this day no one is still quite sure how Lumber
Cats wield their tiny axes. Like all felines, they lack
opposable thumbs.

METAL CAT

SKULLIUS THRASHIUS

ORIGIN

Born in the fires of exploding guitar amps, Metal Cats are typically found roaring dismal lyrics into corroded microphones. They are the original meat-grinding, whisker-bristling, thrash-core metallists. They worship the Dark Lord in addition to worshipping themselves. They are hedonists and nihilists and many more -ists that are too numerous to name here.

BEHAVIOR

Metal Cats brood about their dark pasts and even darker futures. They head-bang until the sky rains blood. They smash guitars and set fire to drumkits. They loudly rehearse their screech-core ballads at 3 a.m. when the Dark Lord is most potent.

WARNING

They will assault your eardrums with unfettered chord-splitting righteousness. They will immolate themselves to light up the stage. They will barricade the doors and burn down an Ed Sheeran concert. They will eat scalding pizza straight out of the oven, just to feel something. They are the shadow that falls over a sullen grave. They are a coagulated blood moon. They are raw. They are loud. They are Metal Cats.

SANTA PAWS

CATTUS FERIAS

ORIGIN

Legend holds that on Christmas Eve, Santa Paws takes off from his Arctic workshop in a magic, toy-laden sleigh to deliver gifts around the world. And also to knock down low-hanging tree ornaments, shred couch corners with his claws, and coat carpets and rugs with cat hair.

PHYSICAL CHARACTERISTICS

Extremely tubby. Since no conventional cat door can accommodate him, Santa Paws usually enters homes through the chimney.

BEHAVIOR

Possibly the only cat in the history of the world who can be accurately described as "jolly."

WARNING

Children who have been good all year round receive delightful presents from Santa Paws, but bad kids get a single, still-warm hairball in their slippers.

YOGA CAT

EXERCITIUM ELIT CATTUS

ORIGIN

All cats are flexible, but the Yoga Cat takes stretchiness to a new level—if not a new plane of existence. A particularly ancient breed, it is said to have inspired the earliest Indian gurus to develop both the philosophy and physical postures associated with modern yogic practices.

PHYSICAL CHARACTERISTICS

The Yoga Cat's joints are extremely elastic, allowing it to assume positions beyond the capabilities not just of humans, but of other felines as well.

HEALTH

It is said that Yoga Cats never truly die, but simply ascend to a higher dimension.

FUN FACT

A small percentage of Yoga Cats develop a mystical third eye in the middle of their foreheads.

IDENTITY
CRISIS
CATS

CATCUS

CACTUS GYMNOCALICIUM CATTUS

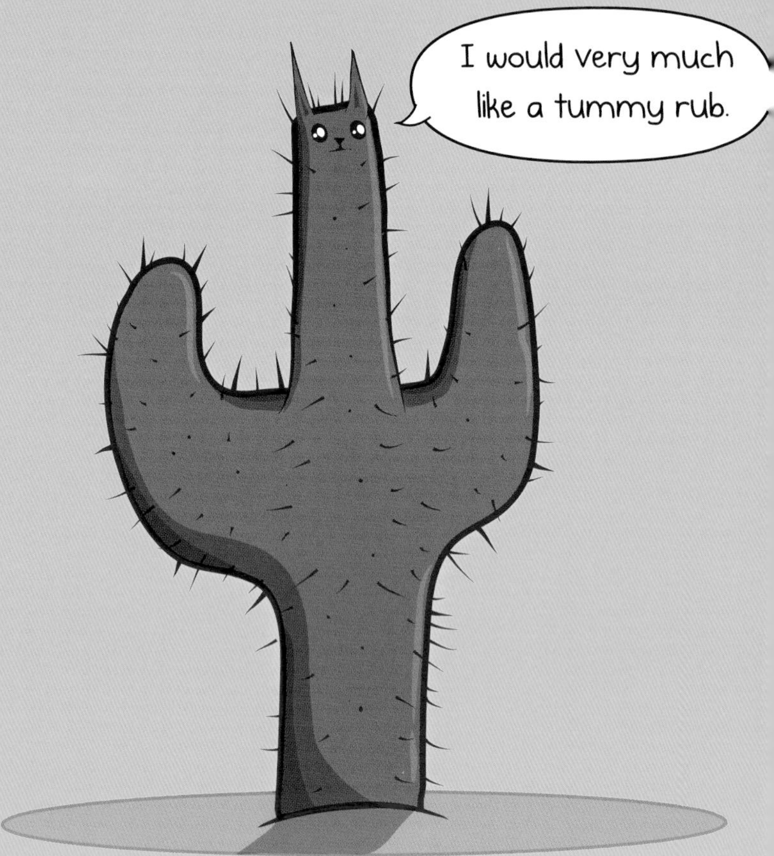
I would very much like a tummy rub.

ORIGIN

Developed by the desert-dwelling tribes of the American Southwest, the Catcus is perfectly adapted to its arid environment. Since they are rooted to the ground, they don't display much in the way of classic catlike behavior. However, they will intently watch any birds that flit by or land on them, they will definitely scratch those that get too close, and they'll purr enthusiastically if their bellies are (carefully) patted.

WARNING

If you make a habit of petting Catcus bellies, you might want to buy a pair of thick leather gloves.

WHERE TO FIND THEM

In arid residential areas, such as Las Vegas, the Catcus serves as both a pet and a landscaping feature.

CATERPILLAR

MOREM PELLIS HISPIDUS CATTUS

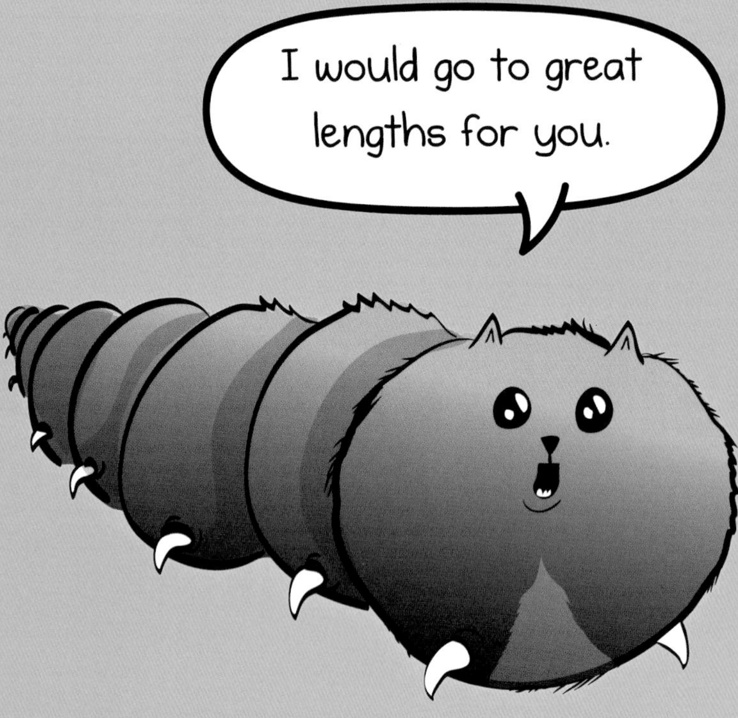
I would go to great lengths for you.

ORIGIN

The Caterpillar's "environment" is confined almost entirely to the leaves of catnip plants, which it gorges on 24/7. It's theorized that this tiny feline formerly cocooned itself in the fall and morphed into a catlike butterfly creature. However, the sheer delight of eating catnip all day caused the Caterpillar to delay its metamorphosis longer and longer, until it finally forgot about it entirely.

PHYSICAL CHARACTERISTICS

Wears a perpetual, dopey smile.

BEHAVIOR

The Caterpillar eats catnip with the single-minded dedication of a stoner working his way through a bag of potato chips.

FUN FACT

Overzealous members of the species will occasionally consume the entire plant on which they live, leaving them no choice but to crash at their parents' catnip plant.

CAT FISH

CATTUS SILURUS

ORIGIN

Known to science only through a handful of fossils, the Cat Fish no doubt was the first catlike creature to emerge from the oceans and walk on land. All of this happened approximately 400 million years ago—slightly after the first recorded terrestrial appearance of the lesser-known Mouse Fish. Fossilized tracks show that the breed already exhibited classic feline traits. Specifically, they would crawl laboriously out of the water, look around, then crawl back into the ocean . . . only to repeat the exact same behavior a few minutes later.

FUN FACT

The Cat Fish's traditional aversion to water apparently fueled its rapid move from sea to land. Once out of the ocean, it quickly evolved into such full-time ground pounders as the fearsome Catasaurus Rex.

CATTERNAUT

SPATIUM CATTUS

ORIGIN

Recruited as test passengers for US spacecraft at
the dawn of the space race, Catternauts proved a less-
than-ideal choice. They routinely ignored instructions,
and their continual shedding played havoc with sensitive
electronic equipment in zero-g environments. But in
spite of these drawbacks, a contingent of Catternauts
is kept on call to this day, mostly for their peerless public
relations skills. To put it simply, they look adorable in
their little spacesuits.

BEHAVIOR

An effervescent mix of good humor and overwhelming
confidence makes Catternauts an extremely popular pet.
Many, after retiring from their government duties, relocate
directly to the homes (and laps) of generals, senators,
and other high-ranking government officials.

WHERE TO FIND THEM

Hanging out at seedy drinking establishments near the
Kennedy Space Center or Edwards Air Force Base.
Catlike creatures with unusually large eyes and almost
no fur have also been sighted at Nevada's Area 51.

CENTAUR CAT

CENTAURUS CATTUS

ORIGIN

Created by the gods to serve as a hero's steed, Centaur Cat instead ignored all instructions and refused to come when called. It's said that the hero it was intended for still follows it forlornly, pleading with it to cooperate so he can begin his quest.

BEHAVIOR

Likes to lick its hooves, squeeze inside large cardboard boxes, and expose its belly to random strangers—whom it then bites if they attempt to rub said belly.

HOME CARE TIP

Needs a very large litter box.

HAT CAT

TOASTIUS CROWNIUS

ORIGIN

Hat Cats are a subspecies of the common house cat. They use human beings as furniture. To them, you are an electric blanket that happens to be self-aware. You are a futon with a metabolism. You are a sofa that says things. You are not destined for greatness—you are destined to be furniture.

WHERE TO FIND THEM

Lounging on your head or face at 4 a.m.

WHERE NOT TO FIND THEM

In that expensive cat bed you bought them.

SLOTH CAT

LAZIUS MAXIMUS

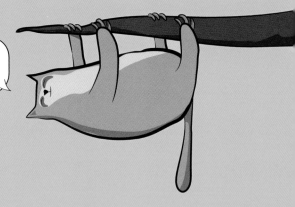

ORIGIN

Sloth Cats originated in the jungles of Central America and eventually found their way into common households, where they spend most of their day napping, dozing, sleeping, and napping again.

BEHAVIOR

Sloth Cats get a bad rap for being slow and lazy, but in reality they differ very little from regular cats. Both sleep all the time. Both contribute very little. Both seem cute and unassuming, while in reality they have subjugated the human race into buying them expensive pillows and bringing them treats.

WHERE TO FIND THEM

If you own a regular cat, look in your own house, because you basically already own a Sloth Cat.

EXPLODING KITTENS is an attractive group of humans who make games for people who are into kittens and explosions and laser beams and sometimes goats. They make a bunch of party games and have sold almost 9 million of them. You should buy their games. They are really fun. Everyone says so.

SAM STALL has authored or co-authored more than 20 books that span the realm of pop culture. Sam lives in Indianapolis with his wife Jami and their son, James.